# Baby Development

*An Essential Guide to Tracking Infant Development and Knowing What to Expect in Your Baby's First Year*

by Carolyn Macaraig

# Table of Contents

# Introduction

The first year of your infant's life is an amazing period. No matter how thrilled you are to meet this cute little bundle for the first time, you may feel a bit nervous too, because you have so many questions about your baby's physical and mental development. It's normal to feel this way. If you have been wondering about how your baby is supposed to grow and progress, and what changes to expect along the way, you can use this guide to assist you and give you the answers you need.

Even new parents typically are aware of the more basic milestones to look forward to, and more precisely, when to expect them. However, besides these – such as sitting, crawling, and standing up – there are lots of other minor milestones that your baby will reach which can be perceived as critical indicators of health and proper development. For instance, you'll witness many unusual and unforeseen nuances, such as your baby's quickening reactions and reflexes, some of which will make you laugh, while others may trouble you a bit. By being well-equipped with information and knowledge, you will know what things are normal and expected within the first year of your baby's life.

Every little success your baby achieves is an amazing event to be celebrated and remembered, from the first time your baby supports the weight of his or her own head, to speaking their very first words. But aside from just being cute, these milestones also provide valuable clues as to your baby's progress in terms of physical and mental development.

Of course there's no need to outright panic if your baby doesn't do the exact things described in this guide at the exact time frame. Keep in mind that each and every one of these little beings is unique, and children develop at their own pace and will typically catch up with each other eventually by going through the similar stages and achieving the same results in the long run.

Working with a knowledgeable pediatrician is absolutely recommended, and no information provided within this book is meant to be a substitute for regular visits with, or any specific information provided by, your pediatrician.

5

# Month 1

Although it's been just a few days, your baby has developed a bond with you. Now that she needs to get used to the surroundings outside the womb, she learns that she can rely on her mommy and daddy. Even though she can't understand your words, your voice is soothing to her and helps her adjust to this new environment.

In the first week, your baby can't do much. However, she is equipped with some reflexes which help babies survive during this initial period of time, until they get used to the new environment. You may recognize one of these when your baby turns her head towards your hand when you try to stroke her cheek because she is actually looking for food. In a week or two, you will also notice this reflex when your baby flings out her arms and legs and then retracts them quickly. Babies usually do this as a response to some sudden movement or noise that startles them, and they typically start to cry. To help avoid this upsetting reaction and allow your baby to remain calm, you can wrap your baby to limit her movements. These reflexes gradually disappear as your baby gains control over her limbs and muscles.

In the second week, the baby will start to focus on faces in close proximity. Babies don't see much when they are born. Their vision is typically blurry, but they can focus on objects about 10 inches away from them. This is actually the distance of your face from your baby's face while breastfeeding. Also, high-contrasting colors are what they can see best and focus on most when their eyesight starts to develop.

At this time, you will be exhausted because your baby's appetite will increase and she will be hungry all the time. You need to prepare for more frequent feeding sessions. As a consequence, your baby will gain some weight, but she will also gain more control over her muscles so that her movements won't be that jerky. When her motions appear to be more controlled, you can start pulling her to a sitting position. Also, somewhere around this time, your baby may experience some colic pain, which may make her cry more. This pain usually occurs due to milk-supply problems, immature digestion, or even environmental factors. What you can do is to check that your baby is not too cold or warm and \ try to calm her in your arms.

Oh, I almost forgot: crying. But you probably already know this, right? Babies seem to cry all the time, but this is their natural means of communication. You may be entertained by a whole repertoire of cries, and when you get to know what these mean, your life will be much easier; it's as simple as that. Other than crying, your baby will also start to discover other ways to use her vocal cords. Thus, you may hear some adorable gurgles, grunts and coos.

When your baby is born, her neck muscles are very weak and that is why she needs you to support her, because she can't support the weight of her head. In a few weeks, your baby will gain a little head control so that she will be able to lift her head a bit and turn her head from side to side. This is an important thing because strong neck muscles will later help your baby sit unassisted, crawl, and walk. In order to develop strong neck muscles, babies need to spend some time each day on their tummies. The floor is the best place for tummy time.

# Month 2

When your baby is born, she is equipped with things for getting your attention. So, besides crying, she starts smiling as well, and she will gradually begin to replace all that crying with cooing, squealing, or gurgling with a gummy smile. Smile and coo back, and your baby will also learn that her actions can cause reactions. Later on, you may hear some laughing as well. She will also discover other sounds that she can make, and these will form the basis of her language skills. Your baby will smile when she sees her mommy and daddy, but also when she hears music (even singing or humming). She is aware of all other sounds as well, and she will react differently to them. Try to recognize those who make her nervous and differentiate them from those who amuse her and calm her down.

At birth, your baby makes movements that are involuntary. As she gradually takes control over her movements in this week, she will discover that she can kick her legs on purpose. She will most certainly kick her legs in the bath to make the water splash, this kicking is actually another way to communicate with you. It may mean that she is tired, excited, or happy when she sees you. Your baby will also improve her coordination and she'll start reaching for things, at this time, that will mostly be your finger or your face, and she will discover her best toys—her toes and fingers. You will also notice how much your baby loves your face. She will follow you with her eyes wherever you go. It is important to spend lots of time with her during this period because this will help her learn how to interact with the world around her faster.

The benefit of all that tummy time is that her neck muscles are becoming stronger. So, continue with tummy time and your baby may be able to do a mini-pushup during these sessions.

When your baby's senses start to develop, your baby will be very busy. You will see how she can connect her rattle with the sound it can make. Also, she will prefer three dimensional objects to flat ones, as well as bright colors to the dull one. Babies learn fast, so you should now help her by surrounding her with lots of opportunities to stimulate her senses and foster learning, but be careful not to overload her.

You will also notice a growth spurt during which your baby may be more fussy than usual. She will also want to be fed more often and longer than usual. This usually lasts for about 3 days.

She may also discover consonants and vocalize something like 'ma' or 'mu'. Your baby will become interested in your talk and you will notice how she looks intently at your mouth as you speak to her. This can be a good time to start reading to her.

# Month 3

Your baby can recognize her parents' faces when in a group. You can't help but notice how her eyes widen and shine when she sees you two. She will learn to maintain eye contact with you and begin to interact socially with the world around. It's not uncommon for babies at this age to be able to read your face and sense when you are sad, happy, angry, etc. She will also recognize her parents' voices and respond with excitement when she sees you. Your baby is also becoming more sensitive to the noise around her. Unexpected noise may upset her. To encourage her to become used to these, you can play her music, read, or talk to her.

Your baby is sleeping less, she is anxious to learn, and alert enough to enjoy some active playtime. Your baby will start to show her interest in a variety of toys, games, and certain activities. Her rattle may not be that interesting to her anymore; rattles and other dangling toys are important for your baby because they help develop her hand-eye coordination. One of the surviving reflexes babies are born with is the ability to hold objects. However, up until now, your baby hasn't been able to do it voluntarily. Also, she'll examine her hands, opening and closing her fingers. She will discover that her hands and fingers are separate objects and so she will look at them, bring them together, even taste them. This is how her hand-eye coordination develops. Both you and your baby will enjoy pram walks, your baby will especially enjoy playing in the light and shade while walking under trees. During that tummy time, your baby will definitely be able to raise herself up on her arms. She may also try to crawl towards you in this position.

The baby will also start to babble, which will be another way of her talking to you. Don't forget to respond in return. Try nursery rhymes and songs. Since babies learn from repetition, don't overload your baby with a variety of these, stick to one or two of these songs. As you've been talking to your baby, she may discover that your speech is broken down in syllables, a pattern she will now use in her attempts to talk. Also, she will be able to laugh, babble, and chuckle in long chains.

Finally, it will appear that your baby has discovered her sleeping routine. She will sleep three times a day for about 2 hours. However, she may wake up in the night for feeding.

# Month 4

Your baby will start rolling over, so it goes without saying that you shouldn't leave your baby unsupervised on a bed or any other high surface. She may roll front to back or back to front. Very frequently, babies can roll only in one direction at first. Rolling over is a sign that your baby has developed strong neck and head muscles. Let your baby roll because it is important for developing the muscles which will later allow her to crawl and sit unassisted.

The baby will learn how to communicate her disapproval. Whatever you do—picking her up, taking her toy away, placing her on her tummy, she will have her opinion about everything. And if she doesn't like something, she will send you a clear message—she will scream, cry, or be fussy. These may be the first glimpses of the baby separating from you and asserting more of her personality.

She will very often try to put toys and other things she can grab in her mouth. This appears to be her favorite way of discovering the world around her. It's not surprising at all because the mouth is a very sensitive area, and it can tell her about the textures, temperature, or shapes of the objects around her that she is trying to understand. This will also teach your baby other oral skills, such as chewing and swallowing food.

By this time, your baby will have learned how to entertain herself. But if she sees you, she will most likely prefer your company. This is an important thing, even if your baby is able to keep herself entertained, even for a few minutes. This will actually teach her to be an independent thinker and to be self-reliant. She will love to play with a mirror; she will need time to understand that she is looking at herself. Babies love this because they discover that there are other babies as well, they then try to chat to this person they see in the mirror. Your baby will also start amusing you with blowing raspberries. During this period, her development is typically focused on developing speech-related skills. By doing this, your baby actually strengths her facial muscles and learns to control her tongue and mouth so that they can work together to produce sounds.

Maybe her first teeth will start to appear. They will probably be the two bottom front teeth, followed by the two upper front teeth. When the baby's first teeth appear, it is important to use a soft cloth to clean them.

# Month 5

She may also start combining consonants, saying things like "dada," "gaga," "mama," or "baba." Although you may feel excited when you hear these words, these are not her first words because they have no meaning to her yet. Basically, she is just playing with syllables. She'll also experiment with sounds as well, so she will play with different sounds, pitch, and volume. She will also discover different sounds by dropping her toys or other objects she can grab to the floor. Now the baby will also start reaching for the objects that are out of her reach and will continue exploring the world with her mouth.

Some babies around this age start to wake up more often during nights for feeding. This happens because they are too active and distracted during the day that they don't give much attention to feeding. During this time, your baby will be on the go. She may creep around and be too busy to play with you. Also, you'll start to notice some traits of her personality. You may get the first glimpses and see if your baby is an adventurer or a laid-back person.

As your baby is learning and getting accustomed to the world around, you will need to find new things or ways to entertain her. Babies learn from repetition, so if you discover some new game, be prepared to play it again and again. While your baby is learning, it is important to reinforce her behavior and efforts. So whenever she does something, encourage her with an excited voice so that she knows that her efforts have been noticed.

By this time, you may also start protecting her teeth by wiping them with a damp soft cloth.

# Month 6

Your baby has developed her upper body strength and coordination, but now her lower body faces a challenge. At this time, your baby should be steadier when sitting up on her own, although she may still need your help now and again. You'll notice that her head and neck muscles are stronger, so she can now keep her head level when you pull her into a sitting position.

You may also notice that your baby is all of a sudden afraid of strangers, i.e. people she doesn't see daily. This happens because the memory for faces of your baby has improved a bit so she can tell familiar from unfamiliar people. Just as your baby is afraid of strangers, she also fears a physical separation from you.

By this time your baby can recognize names, familiar sounds, and some basic words like "no" or "bye-bye."

Also, some babies may be able to point to the objects you call. This is called receptive language, and it actually precedes the ability to speak. You can also expect to hear some speech-like sounds. She will begin to learn turn-taking in conversation as you wait for her babble to stop, so that you can "answer" her. You can encourage her conversation with you by imitating the sounds she makes. She may even produce a range of sounds and tones that she may not ordinarily hear. Continue reading to your baby. It doesn't matter what you read to her because it's the tone of your voice that's important to her at this age.

Somewhere around this time, you can change your baby's diet and start giving her solid food. Your baby may not like it at first because she needs time to get used to the new textures and tastes. Generally, you should avoid seasoning her food and offering her sweet food. When you introduce solid food to your baby's diet, it doesn't mean that you should all of a sudden stop breastfeeding her. Weaning happens over months, and to help you with this, you should always offer your baby solid foods when she is really hungry, then breastfeed her. In that way, she will take less milk and more solid foods.

Around this time, your baby should be able to sleep for 8 hours without waking during the night to be fed.

# Month 7

Your baby will be learning about cause and effect by again dropping things. She will drop things all around and wait for you to pick them up for her. Also, she will learn to predict some of your responses, for example, you will smile back when she smiles at you.

Your baby finally can sit up by herself. In the beginning, she may need to support herself with one of her arms because sitting is challenging for her since she needs to hold her head, neck, spine, and shoulders erect; she also needs to learn how to balance her weight evenly. After so many failed attempts, she can finally do it; and after a couple of weeks, she will no longer need to support herself. After learning how to sit, your baby will begin to find different ways to move around in no time, this will help develop her muscular strength and coordination, which will later help her crawl. Some babies even creep backwards because their upper body is stronger than their lower body.

Your baby has developed her gross motor skills, such as head control, kicking, creeping, and sitting; now comes the time to develop some of her fine motor skills. She can now use her hands in a more sophisticated way. She may clap her hands, for instance, or she may also start feeding herself. Your baby will also begin to pick up smaller objects and try to pass them from one hand to the other. You can start teaching her how to hold her cup and sip from it.

Her memory will improve as well, so that now she can recall some experiences shortly after they have happened. This will enable her to be more determined about what she wants, so that for instance, she will imitate actions she has already seen. Moreover, this will enable her to anticipate certain activities, such as bath time, bed time, lunch, etc. You'll also notice her new interest in toys which have doors or buttons that she can press.

She will also develop some more sophisticated ways of socializing. She'll enjoy finding the object you have hidden for her to find, peek-a-boo will be one of her favorite games.

You will also notice how her leg muscles are now stronger so that she can bear her own weight, which is an important step to walking. Be prepared though, because standing may easily become her preferred position.

# Month 8

After learning how to crawl, it's only a matter of time before she learns how to stand up. She may use some furniture or you to help her stand up. Don't be surprised if she suddenly falls down while standing. Some babies don't crawl but go from sitting to walking, whereas other babies need more time to master crawling. Some babies spend time rocking back and forth on their hands and knees until they figure out how to use their body to move forward.

Your baby is also beginning to understand object permanence. What does this mean? Well, the baby understands that even though she can't see them, objects exist and these objects, which she can only partially see, have hidden elements. Also, she will discover that you have not disappeared completely even though you have left the room. The world around her has expanded dramatically, thus her concentration suddenly increases as well. She becomes curious about the environment. Peek-a-boo is a great game for this period, now that she understands object permanence.

You'll also discover that she now understands or recognizes her name. In that sense, your communication will be easier because you will be able to get her attention by calling her name. Also, the baby begins to understand the meaning of the word "no." She will pause with the activity she is doing and look at you to see how serious you are when she hears this word.

If you listen carefully, you may hear the rhythm of speech in her babble. She will begin to combine consonants and vowels to resemble speech. Also, she will be able to understand some basic words, so you should label things for and read lots of books to her.

# Month 9

She will work on developing her fine motor skills, so the first thing she will learn is probably passing a toy from one hand to the other without dropping it. By this time, she will need to develop sufficient hand-eye coordination to perform this task. By now, your baby may be able to feed herself. At this time, you may also be showered with lots of hugs and kisses—another milestone in your baby's development to be remembered.

Your baby is more curious than ever before, so make sure that she is safe all the times. She wants to learn about the world around her and how things in this world work. Thus, she will take things out of shelves and cabinets and leave them out. She will explore sounds by banging objects together to see what kind of noises they make. Your baby will learn from simple activities you do every day. You'll notice how your baby watches your every move and even tries to imitate you because this is her way of learning. Also, around this time, your baby may show a preference for toys which resemble real-life objects. Your baby will still put objects into her mouth to explore the world.

As your baby is now able to understand some simple words, it is more important than ever to talk to her and encourage her to repeat some of the words she can hear. Her first attempts will be far away from your version, but encourage her to keep trying.

# Month 10

Somewhere around this time, your baby will develop her social skills—she will learn to wave goodbye, which is important because she will understand this element of social interaction, that when you leave someone's company, you may give them a kiss or simply wave goodbye. This is also important because she will begin to understand social cues.

Your baby is now on-the-go, discovering new ways of moving faster; and about now, your baby will be able to stand alone. She will pull herself up using furniture as a support and then let go of it, or she may first sit on her haunches and then move onto her feet and then straighten her legs. Now that your baby can stand up alone, it's only a matter of time before she will start cruising around the furniture. She will be able to move around by holding on to furniture and other objects to maintain her balance.

You may discover how all of a sudden your baby is afraid of almost everything, even things that she liked before. Her greatest fear may come from loud noises. This fear is actually good, it means that your baby has started to understand that there are dangers in this world which have to be avoided.

You may also notice that your baby gets frustrated when she can't communicate what she wants.

# Month 11

Now that your baby is becoming more sociable, after so many days spent watching at and trying to imitate you, she will want to help you and engage in the same activities as you do. Although she may be distracting you more than helping you, don't discourage her, because this is another way for her to learn. Somewhere around this time, your baby may appear to be shy. This happens because she is becoming more socially aware and thus this makes her wary of new and unfamiliar social experiences. It's not good to label your baby as shy, because she can carry this into adulthood. Instead, give her time to get comfortable and feel confident enough to explore these new situations.

Once your baby has understood object permanence, she can move on to problem-solving. There are lots of toys which are great for your baby at this age that require lots of concentration. Your baby may also want to be independent while doing certain tasks, and refuse your help, even when she needs it. Don't be surprised if your baby starts expressing her opinions.

That little being knows what she likes and what she doesn't, and she is not afraid to express that loud and clear. Somewhere around this time, your baby may be a bit picky when it comes to foods she eats, sometimes even rejecting her favorites. Moreover, she may start whining to get things she wants. When this starts happening, you need to set some limits, and once you say "no," don't give in. Also, as your baby has a couple of teeth, she may discover that she can use them to bite. She will probably bite you first and you should discourage this behavior immediately. However, you should not react strongly and in a high-pitched voice because babies associate this with excitement.

She may have started grabbing smaller objects using her index and thumb, but by this time she may have developed a strong grip. This means that she will be able to play with a greater variety of toys because she will be able to twist and turn small parts of toys. This will also help her feed herself as she will be able to pick up some finger foods. It's not at all surprising that with the ability to move around and pick up small objects, she will try to eat things that are not food. Try to minimize the risk of this kind of behavior to keep your baby safe.

# Conclusion:  Happy Birthday!

While she appears to want to be independent, her feelings of insecurity may creep in again. She may again feel anxious around strangers. When this happens, stay close to her when she needs you. Since her imagination is developing quickly, she may not like being in her bed all alone and will try to keep you by her side.

By this time, your baby should sleep twice a day. But during the next few weeks you may notice how this mid-afternoon sleep is not when it should be, but about 5pm or even later; this may affect her sleep at night. If this starts to happen, you may try to limit the amount of time she spends sleeping during the day.

By now, your baby may have a few words in her vocabulary that she knows the meaning of. Now is the right time to expand her vocabulary quickly because she has a better control over her mouth, tongue, and palate. Your baby will use words in isolation and will know to change her tone of voice to ask you a question. Encourage her interest in language by speaking clearly and slowly.

She may also begin to enjoy playing with other kids. However, she won't be willing to share, and as she still can't communicate, she will use the same methods she uses with objects in her surroundings. So, she may try to pull their hair, bite them, or try to kiss them. Your baby will also start to learn how to handle different objects, for instance you may notice how she tucks a toy under her arm to grab another.

Your baby will start trying to walk on her own although most babies achieve this when they are 13-months old. She may try to let go of your hands and furniture for a few seconds and try to make a step or two before she falls down. She will continue trying this, and it won't take long before she eventually masters this trick. In any case, your baby will only start to walk the moment she feels so inclined, no matter how much you encourage her to start doing it earlier.

Finally, I'd like to thank you for purchasing this book! If you enjoyed it or found it helpful, I'd greatly appreciate it if you'd take a moment to leave a review on Amazon. Thank you!

86565540R00035

Made in the USA
Middletown, DE
30 August 2018